The St Swithun's Way

A Guide to the Walk
From
Farnham
To
Winchester

By
Bob Brunt

The St Swithun's Way

Contents

Introduction

Introduction

The Saint Swithun's Way is a long distance walking trail being approximately 34 miles (53 kilometres) long running from Farnham Station to Winchester Cathedral. The walk was originally opened in 2002 by Hampshire County Council.

The St Swithun's Way is designed to follow the mediaeval pilgrimage routes between Winchester and Canterbury linking (at Farnham) with the North Downs Way to Canterbury and Dover.

The routes taken by pilgrims walking between Winchester and Canterbury are not formally recorded but it is considered likely they would have followed old routes such as Roman roads or drove roads.

Part of the route near Alton does follow the old Roman roads for a short distance.

As well as linking with the North Downs Way the St Swithun's way also links to the South Downs Way which is another national trail of approximately 100 miles from Winchester to Eastbourne in Sussex.

The Saint Swithun's Way starts near Farnham Station and passes close to 2 rivers, the River Wey between Farnham and Alton and the River Itchen near Winchester.

The Way also passes through several villages with thatched cottages and churches many of which have been on the site for centuries.

Outside Alton the way follows the disused Alton to Fareham railway line for a short distance.

Whilst walking along the way there several country pubs both on and just off the route that can be visited for refreshments.

At Farnham there is the Farnham Museum or Farnham Castle both can be visited.

In Alton there are museums such as The Curtis Musuem and the Allen Gallery.

At Chawton the route passes the house where between 1809 and 1817 Jane Austen lived with her mother and her sister Cassandra.

At the market town of Alresford, just off the route you can take a ride on the (seasonal) steam railway known as the Watercress Line, which runs between Alresford and Alton. At Alresford the Way passes by some of the watercress beds which gives the railway its name.

In the ancient Saxon capital of England Winchester there are numerous places of interest including the Cathedral. More details of the places of interest are included in the sections of each proposed days walk.

The St Swithun's Way can be walked easily over 3 days the distance and time taken is entirely up to the individual walker and some may to wish to take longer or shorter walks depending on the weather conditions and the fitness of the walker.
In writing this book I have used the 3 day choice as I personally feel this is the most comfortable.
I have, in each stage, included a chart giving the approximate distances between parts of this walk this could be helpful in allowing the walker to plan their own itinerary.
The suggested routes are between Farnham and Alton approximately 19 Kilometres (12 miles), Alton and Alresford approximately 19 Kilometres (12 miles) and Alresford and Winchester approximately 14 km (9 miles). Again in each stage I have produced sketch maps showing the route and nearby villages. It should be noted the sketch maps used in this book are for guidance purpose only.

The maps are based on the Ordnance Survey Landranger maps series but it is strongly recommended that you should carry a copy of either the Landranger series or the Explorer series of maps covering the walks.

A compass might also be helpful but not essential as you are never far away from "civilisation".

The information in this book is correct as at 2104 when I walked the route. Unfortunately things often change and not necessarily for the better and you may find variations of the route or some of the places such as the pubs are no longer trading. For example only a few weeks after I walked through the village of Ropley the village church was almost totally destroyed by a major fire.

I hope this book encourages you to decide to walk the St Swithun's Way and wish you some happy days walking if you do so.

St Swithun

The Saint Swithun's Way is dedicated to a Saxon Bishop of Winchester.

Believed to be born around the year 800 AD, Swithun was an educated man and was a tutor to both King Alfred the Great and his father Aethelwulf of Wessex.

Aethelwulf rewarded Swithun by appointing him as Bishop of Winchester in 852AD.

As Bishop of Winchester Swithun is believed to have been involved in the building of the East Gate Bridge in Winchester.

When Swithun died on 2nd July 862 he made a request that he should not to be buried within the church, but outside in a common grave.

After his death Swithun was popular and many miracles were attributed to him resulting in his sainthood.

Sometime after his death Swithun's remains were moved into the church against his wishes and immediately afterwards there was a prolonged period of bad weather which probably resulted in the traditional well known poem:

St Swithun's Day, if thou dost rain, For forty days it will remain;
St Swithun's Day, if thou be fair, For forty days 'twill rain nae mair.

The St Swithun's Way
Day 1
Farnham to Alton
19.8 Km 12.3 miles

Key to Maps

St Swithun's Way

Other Footpath or Bridleway

A Road or Motorway

Railway

B Road or country lane

Residential Road

River Itchen

PH   Public House

Take Care (busy or dangerous road)

The St Swithuns Way

Map 1

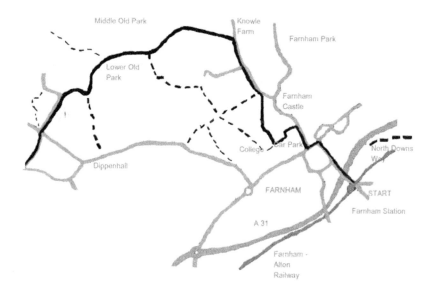

Approximate Elevations

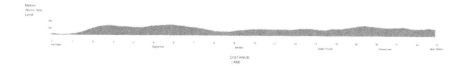

Day 1
Farnham Station to Alton

Farnham Station is the start of the North Downs Way a national trail of over 100 miles to Dover and Canterbury. From here you can follow the possible pilgrim's route down to Canterbury Cathedral.

At Farnham Station head downhill to the busy A31 and cross over by the traffic lights to enter South Street. Continue straight on to the crossroads by Barclays Bank and cross over the road here and immediately turn left.

Cross over Castle Street and immediately turn right following this road slightly uphill. Look out for a St Swithun's Way marker on a lamp post (after approximately 150 metres) and turn left to enter a narrow alleyway. At the end of the alley turn left and then right and follow the path which arrives at a car park which is on your right.

Enter the car park and head slightly uphill to a visible footpath in the top right corner. The path continues to climb and turns left. At a junction (with the Institute of Art on your left) turn right to enter a field and continue to climb.

The main path normally goes straight across this field but on occasions during the farming seasons it can be diverted to go around the edge of the field.

The path leaves the field and passes along an enclosed path between gardens of houses before it emerges on to a quiet road. Turn left and follow this road which turns to the right. Ignore the first footpath off to the left and continue for approximately 1 kilometre to a junction where you turn left (look out for St Swithun's markers) continue to follow this road for approximately 400 metres where after passing some houses the road becomes a track which enters woodland.

The track exits the wood and emerges onto another tarmac lane which you continue to follow ignoring footpaths off to the left and right.

The lane passes houses and winds gently round and eventually climbs to join a busier road on a bend. Turn left at the junction to join this new road.

Take care as there is no pavement and the road can be very busy carrying all types of traffic.

The St Swithuns Way

Follow this road for approximately 300 metres to arrive at an offset crossroads, which is located on the Surrey and Hampshire border, turn left and cross the road (with care) to turn right immediately into a much quieter country lane which climbs gently. There are views back towards Farnham from here. Continue along this lane for some distance until you reach a junction at Dippenhall Farm.

Cross directly over the road to join a farm track which now meanders between fields.

The track emerges onto a narrow lane with a St Swithun's Mile post on your right showing you have already walked 4 miles.

The St Swithuns Way

Cross directly over the lane to join a field edge path opposite.

After a short while this path enters woods and eventually emerges onto a lane.

Turn left and after approximately 75 metres turn right to pass by a gate to follow a path which crosses a field and then drops downhill towards a wood.

At the bottom of the hill cross over a sleeper bridge and turn right and left at the next path to enter the woods along a wide track.

Follow the track through the woods. Near the edge of the woodland the path turns left and passes by a gate before emerging onto a tarmac lane. Turn left here and at the next junction turn right to follow the lane past some cottages. *Look right immediately for the stile*

At the next road junction keep straight on to cross a stile and enter a series of fields containing horses. Cross directly over the paddocks going through a mixture of gates and stiles. After passing through this area cross a stile and head diagonally right slightly downhill and then climb to enter a path which runs round the edge of a field to emerge on a road.

Map 2

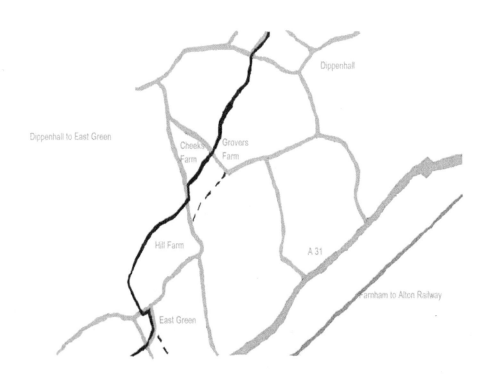

Dippenhall

Dippenhall to East Green

Cheeks Farm   Grovers Farm

Hill Farm   A 31

Farnham to Alton Railway

East Green

The St Swithuns Way

Turn left here to follow this road into the village of Bentley.
At a T Junction continue straight on.
If you wish to visit the Star at Bentley turn left here and walk up to main road and then right again.
At the next junction turn right to walk uphill towards the church. Just before reaching the church turn left to walk along Church Lane and at the end of the lane turn right and after a few metres turn left to pass directly in front of houses before joining a narrow path running alongside fields.

Map 3

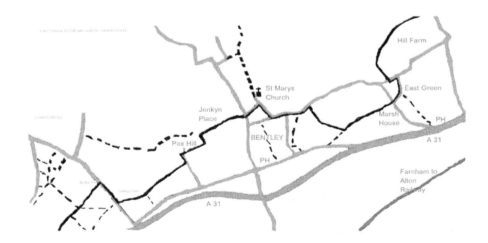

The St Swithuns Way

At a paddock area the path turns left then, immediately before the next paddock, right to pass through a gate and entering a woodland path. At the end of this path the way emerges onto the driveway of Pax Hill where it turns left.

The St Swithun's Way follows the driveway for approximately 150 metres where just before a house turns right to cross a stile to enter a large field.

The route is clear across this field and even in wet weather is easy going.

On the far side of the field the path enters woodland then emerges on to a driveway to Coldrey Farm.

Continue to follow this and turn slightly left to pass by some houses to emerge on a road where you turn right.

Continue along the road until you reach the Anchor public house and restaurant. Immediately before the Anchor turn left to join a field edge path.

The path turns right to cross a sleeper bridge and then almost immediately left to pass between fields.

At a gate turn right and after 30 metres cross a stile to join a tarmac lane leading towards Treloar School.

Look out for a stile on the right, cross this to head directly across the middle of a field towards a second stile which is by a thatched cottage.

Turn left to follow the road through the village of Upper Froyle. Where a road comes in from the right continue straight on and again at the next junction where the road comes in from the left.

Should you wish to visit the Hen and Chicken Public House at Upper Froyle turn left here and follow the road to the main A31.

The route enters a small industrial estate where at a fork you should keep left following the road downhill shortly passing a classic car refurbishment workshop.

The lane now becomes a farm track, at the next fork keep left to join a narrower path which enters a wooded path dropping more steeply downhill and passing a small lake on the left.

The path now climbs then crosses the middle of a large field, passing under power lines, heading towards a copse visible on the far side of the field.

On reaching the trees the path passes through the woods and turns left to follow a field side path.

The way now follows the route of an old Roman road (from Alton) and this can be seen to the left.

The St Swithuns Way

Map 4

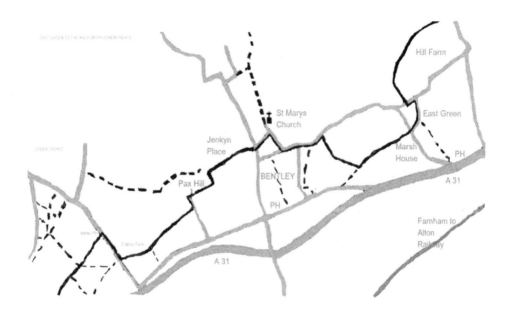

Map 5

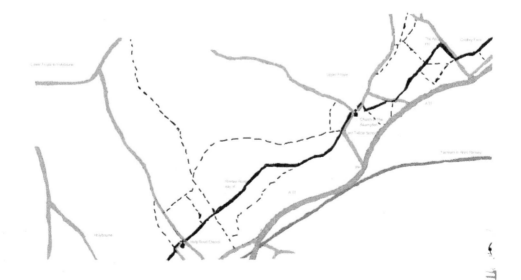

The St Swithuns Way

The path drops downhill and at a gap in the trees crosses over the roman road to continue along the opposite side. The raised roman road ends here the path now drops down to enter and cross a field, still continuing the same line of direction. After crossing a further 2 fields the St Swithun's Way joins a field side path which narrows to run alongside a wall before emerging onto a lane at a T junction with Holybourne Church directly opposite.

The route continues straight on passing to the right of the church. The road turns left and immediately after the first house the St Swithun's Way turns right to join a narrow path.

Map 6

The St Swithuns Way

Continue straight on to pass through a school car park to join another narrow path that runs behind school buildings and playing fields.

At the end of the chain link fence turn left and continue to follow the path which runs between the fence and a row of trees. Just before the end of the fence turn right to head directly across sports fields, passing between pitches, towards houses which can be seen on the far side.

On reaching the far side of the sports field (look out for an exit through the hedge) cross over the road and join the path through residential areas directly opposite.

Continue straight on along the paved paths between and in front of houses until arriving at some garages and a road.

Cross the road and turn left then at the T junction turn right to walk into Alton town centre.

If required Alton Station is a short distance away off to the left. From here there are both trains and buses back to Farnham.

Approximate distances

From - to	Miles	Km	Cumulative Total Miles	Cumulative Total Km
Farnham Station to Dippenhall	3.1	5.0	3.1	5.0
Dippenhall to Bentley	2.6	4.1	5.7	9.1
Bentley to Upper Froyle	2.6	4.1	8.3	13.2
Upper Froyle (Lord Mayor Treeloar College) to Holybourne Church	1.8	3.0	10.1	16.2
Holybourne Church to Alton Town Centre (High Street)	2.2	3.6	12.3	19.8
Day 1 Total Distance			**12.3**	**19.8**

Farnham to Alton Refreshments

On Route	Off Route
Choice of shops, pubs, cafes and restaurants in Farnham	
	The Bull Inn Bentley (on A31)
	The Star Inn in Bentley village
The Anchor at Lower Froyle	
	Hen and Chicken at Upper Froyle(on A31)
	The White Hart In Holybourne
Choice of shops, pubs cafes and restaurants in Alton	

Farnham to Alton

Places of Interest and History

The Surrey town of Farnham located approximately 55km or 35 miles from London. The town is on the border with Hampshire and is approximately 45km (28 miles) from Winchester and located on the main route from Winchester to London that was historically used by the Bishops of Winchester.

The town contains many Georgian houses and just to the North of the town is Farnham Castle and Farnham Park.

Farnham Castle was originally built in 1138 by a Henry De Blois a Bishop of Winchester under the rule of Henry I.

When Henry II took the throne he ordered that the castles built by De Blois be pulled down and the original castle was demolished in 1155. It was rebuilt in the early 13th Century.

The castle was used by the Bishops of Winchester for the several centuries.

During the civil war in the 17th Century the castle was involved in some skirmishes and was partially demolished on Oliver Cromwell's orders. However, after the war the castle underwent changes with more buildings being added to the castle by Bishop George Morley.
In the Second World War the castle was used by the military as a training centre for subterfuge.

Farnham has a history which can be traced back to the Stone Age with evidence of early settlements including Bronze Age relics having been found near the town.

There are 2 known Iron Age hill forts near to the town including an area known as Caesar's Camp which is approximately 3km north of the town.

It is believed that during the Roman period the area around the town was used for the making of pottery.

Farnham is recorded in the 1086 Domesday Book as Ferneham as part of the Diocese of Winchester.

In 1249 the then Bishop of Winchester granted the town its charter.

The Museum of Farnham is located in an 18th century building along West Street and this houses several artifacts covering much of the local area and its history.

The next village on the route is Bentley. This was the location of a radio 4 programme and later TV docu-drama called The Village which was first broadcast during the 1990s and ran for several series.

At Bentley there is the first of several churches which are passed along the Way. The Church of St Mary has parts constructed in the 12th century. The church was rebuilt in 1890   by a Henry Woodyer.

At Coldrey Farm there was a manor which again was in the ownership of the Bishop of Winchester. Parts of the current farm building, which is a private residence, date back to the 14th century.

From Coldrey the Way passes through the village of Upper Froyle. Just before entering the village the route follows an old driveway leading to impressive buildings which now form the Lord Treloar School, a special school for disabled pupils.
This was was set up in 1907 by Sir William Purdie who was a Lord Mayor of London.
The school moved into the buildings at Froyle in 1953. There is also a second part of the school known as Treloar College which is located near Holybourne and this is also passed by the St Swithun's Way.
At Froyle there is the second of the ancient churches. St Marys of the Assumption Church in Upper Froyle was originally constructed in the early 14th Century.
There was however records of a church in the area recorded in the Domesday Book.
The current church has been subject to several refurbishments in the 18th and 19th centuries.

On Leaving Froyle the Way passes alongside the route of an old Roman road. In 1971 a Roman Settlement was discovered near to Alton on the road which ran from Silchester to Chichester in Sussex.

The route of the Roman road leads directly to the village Church of Holy Rood at Holybourne. Again, this village is recorded in the Domesday Book.
The village church has parts dating back to the 12th century. It was rebuilt in 1879.
The church has 8 bells which have been inscribed and dedicated to former residents of Hampshire. The bells are dedicated to the following:

Jane Austen,
Elizabeth Gaskill,
William Curtis,
Alfred Munnings,
Edmund Spenser,
Edward Thomas,
Izaak Walton
and Rev Gilbert White.

The St Swithuns Way

The Market Town of Alton is the next place to be visited.

The town is known for the brutal murder of a young girl forever known as Sweet Fanny Adams.

On 24th August 1867 Frederick Baker, a solicitors clerk who worked in Alton, took the 8 year old Fanny Adams into a hop field near Alton and brutally murdered and dismembered her. The case caused shock and horror throughout the country.
Around about the same time the Royal Navy issued sailors with tins of meat the contents of which were not popular and it was nicknamed Sweet Fanny Adams or Sweet FA.

The town of Alton has a roman settlement known as Vindomis and was on the Chichester to Silchester road.

The Town was also a Saxon settlement and appears in the Domesday Book under the name of Aoltone.

During the English Civil War a small royalist force led by Sir Richard Bolle were outnumbered by a parliamentarian force of 5000 men.
Many of Bolle,s men made a last stand at the Church of St Lawrence just off the High Street. Bolle and most of his men were killed in the battle within the church and its grounds. The church is reputed to still show scars of this battle.

The St Swithun's Way
Day 2
Alton to The Ship Inn
Nr New Alresford
19.4 Km 12.2 miles

Elevations
Alton to The Ship Inn

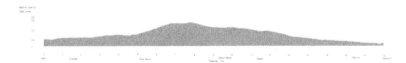

Day 2
Alton to the Ship Inn Nr New Alresford

The second day is an easy walk of around 19 kilometres (12.2 Miles).

The walk starts in Alton and continues along the High Street from Alton Station. *It is best to remain on the north side of the street to avoid the one way systems in the town which can be misleading.*

The way passes directly through the retail area of the town and some of the bus stop shelters have some detail of the St Swithuns way with maps upon them.

After passing through the retail area the way continues straight on and now enters a residential part of the town.

At a fork with a large green known as The Butts keep left staying alongside the main road.

The path passes under a railway bridge and immediately crosses a road (take care this road can be busy at times) in front of a second bridge.

The way continues straight on along a road which passes between the A31 and the railway.

This road passes several industrial units and heads away from the railway. Towards the end of the road it swings right and passes under the A31 by a subway and after a short distance enters the village of Chawton.

The path continues straight on passing through the village and directly in front of Jane Austen's old house, which is now a museum dedicated to the author and her time in the village.

At a junction directly after the house continue straight on passing by some thatched houses.

Shortly after these there are a group of more modern houses set back from the road and the route turns right here to cross a stile and join an enclosed field edge path to the left of these houses.

The path crosses a second stile and drops down to a busy road which is crossed with extreme care to join a path directly opposite.

This path crosses over a field and swings slowly left to join a wider path which heads straight towards an avenue of trees. This is the old Alton to Fareham (Meon Valley) railway line which was closed in 1955.

The way continues along the disused railway passing under an old bridge then at a cross roads of paths (by farm buildings) turns right onto a wide farm track.

At the next junction by a hedgerow the path turns sharply left to join another farm track. The track emerges onto a narrow country lane where the St Swithun's Way now turns right and climbs gently uphill following the lane. The lane passes several farm buildings and houses then becomes a narrower unmade track which enters woods.

The track continues straight on for several hundred metres running along the outer edge of the woodland with fields sometimes visible to the left.
At a T-Junction the way turns right continuing along the unmade tracks in the woodland. Eventually the path arrives at a crossroad of paths and a parking area where the route turns left to enter a residential area in the village of Four Marks.

After a short distance there is a crossroads where the route continues to head straight on along a wide residential lane.

After approximately 300 metres, just after a small garden centre, the route turns left to leave the lane to join a field side path.

After another 300 metres the way turns right crossing a stile to join an enclosed field edge path which drops downhill. At the bottom of the hill the path turns right and after a short distance left to cross another stile then over a country lane to join another field edge path (slightly right) opposite.

The path climbs as it heads along the left side of the grassy field then turns right to enter a second field where it continues straight before entering a third field where it turns left heading towards the left of a house where it joins a narrow path between houses.

After a short distance the path emerges onto a lane near a road junction.

The St Swithun's Way turns right at the lane and crosses the junction to a stile opposite where the path now heads straight across the middle of a field heading towards Old Down Wood.

The path enters the wood by another stile and initially head straight on at a junction of paths the St Swithun's Way turns left to follow a wide path through the woods, which at certain times of the year can be spectacular and covered in bluebells.

At a crossroads of paths continue straight on to follow the path, which now swings right, continuing through the woods but now more on the far edge.

The path eventually emerges from the wood and turns left to head downhill. Initially the wood is on your left but after a short distance the path crosses a stile to continue downhill along a field edge between fields.

After crossing a second field and 2 more stiles the path emerges onto a road opposite a large house where the path follows a farm track to the left of the house directly opposite.

After a few yards the St Swithun's Way turns right to cross a stile and enter a field which it crosses diagonally heading up hill towards a gap in the hedgerow.

The route passes over a further stile in the hedgerow to enter another field which is crossed diagonally.

The route is poorly waymarked here and it can be easy to get lost but generally you should continue straight on, continuing the diagonal route, over the next 4 fields, some of which may be ploughed or full of arable stock, to reach a narrow path which emerges onto a road in the pretty village of Ropley.

On reaching the road the route turns right to pass through the village and the Church of St Peter.

Unfortunately, about a month after I walked through this Norman church was destroyed by a major fire and, at the time of writing, it is not known if it can be re-built.

Ignore the first 2 roads to the left and at the third turn left to head slightly downhill to reach a T-Junction where you turn right.

After a few yards turn left along a sometimes overgrown narrow footpath which shortly arrives onto another road. Continue straight on and follow the road passing several houses.

Where the road swings left look out for a path on the right which steps up into a field which is crossed diagonally heading towards a hedgerow.

After passing through the hedgerow the path continues diagonally across a second field to reach a narrow country lane where it turns right to following the route of the lane.

The lane is followed for some distance as it climbs and turns through the countryside.

Eventually the lane drops slightly down to reach Manor House Farm where it turns right to follow a busier road.

After approximately 250 metres the Way crosses the A 31 (take care) at a roundabout then continues along the road opposite heading towards New Alresford.

After approximately 75 metres the route turns right to join a track then after a further 20 metres turns left to join a sometimes overgrown field edge path which heads straight along the field edge towards some houses which can be seen in the distance.
Continue straight on to the left of the houses to emerge onto a quite lane which crosses over a ford by a bridge.

Continue along this lane which emerges back onto the road to New Alresford then turn right to follow this road which after a short distance arrives at the Ship Inn.

At the Ship Inn there are bus stops where the 64 bus can be taken to get to either Alton or Winchester. The bus normally runs every hour but there is a less frequent service (every 2 hours) on Sundays.

Should you wish to continue into New Alresford you should continue along the road for approximately 2 kilometres.

The Watercress Railway runs from here to Alton. This is a heritage railway running steam trains and is seasonal in operation. Checks should be made before visiting to ensure there is a service on the days you are visiting.

Approximate distances

From - to	Miles	Km	Cumulative Total Miles	Cumulative Total Km
Day 1 Total Distance			**12.3**	**19.8**
Alton town centre to Chawton (Jane Austen's House)	0.9	1.4	13.2	21.2
(Jane Austen's House) Chawton to Four Marks Garden Centre to	3.3	5.3	16.5	26.5
Four Marks Garden Centre to Gilbert Street	2.5	4.0	19.0	30.5
Gilbert Street to Ropley (St Peters Church)	0.8	1.2	19.8	31.7
St Peter's Church Ropley to Ship Inn Bishops Sutton	3.1	5.0	22.9	36.7
Ship Inn Bishop's Sutton to Cricketers Alresford	1.6	2.5	24.5	39.2
Day 2 total Distance			**12.2**	**19.4**

Alton to Bishops Sutton

Refreshments

On Route	Off Route
Day 2	**Day 2**
Choice of shops, pubs cafes and restaurants in Alton	
French Horn The Butts Alton (just off route)	
Greyfriars PH and Cassandra Tea Room at Chawton	
	The Pheasant Lower Farringdon
Four Marks Garden Centre (soft drinks)	
	The Windmill Four Marks (Now Closed)
Ship Inn at Bishops Sutton .	

Alton to Bishops Sutton
Places of Interest and History

Alton Station is the start of the Watercress Line which was previously known as the Mid-Hants Railway which ran between Alton and Winchester. The full line was closed by British Railways in 1973.

In 1985 the full heritage railway line between Alton and New Alresford was opened, shorter lines between stations had been opened previously.

The Watercress line is now approximately 16 kilometres (10 miles) long and is a seasonal railway running steam and diesel locomotives along the route. Alresford was a major producer of watercress which was transferred by rail to London along the line via Alton and the line was subsequently nicknamed the Watercress Line which remains in place today.

There are 2 other stations along the line Four Marks & Medstead and Ropley.

The St Swithun's Way passes through the village of Chawton which is located on the far side of the A31 from Alton.

This village was the home of the author Jane Austen who lived here for the last 8 years of her life before moving to Winchester shortly before she died.

Jane is buried in Winchester Cathedral. Her mother and sister who lived with her in Chawton are buried in the churchyard in the village. In the centre of the village is Chawton Cottage the former home of Jane Austen, this is now a museum dedicated to the author and her time in the village.
Also in the village is Chawton House this is a restored Elizabethan Manor House which was once owned by Jane Austens' brother.
This building is now the centre for the study of Early English Women's Writing and contains a library of over 9000 volumes dated from the early 17th century to the mid -19th century.

After leaving Chawton the St Swithun's Way follows the old course of the Meon Valley Railway.
This ran for 36 kilometres (22 miles) between Alton and Fareham and was opened in 1903.
The line was closed to passenger traffic in 1955 and closed completely in 1968. Much of the route is now a foot and cycle path.

The village of Ropley is situated 4 miles from Alresford. The village contains many old buildings many dating back to the 16th century.
The Church of St Peter in the centre of the village had parts of the building which dated back to the Norman period.
Unfortunately, a couple of months after I walked through the village the church suffered a major fire which destroyed the roof of the building and severely damaged the structure.

The St Swithun's Way
Day 3
The Ship Inn
Nr New Alresford
To
Winchester Cathedral
14.2 Km 8.9 miles

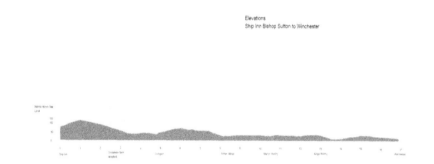

Day 3
Ship Inn to Winchester Cathedral

Much of the walk on the final day is on tarmac along roads and country lanes and care should be taken as some vehicles can approach at speed.

From the Ship Inn take the first road on the right (approximately 30 metres from the pub). At an early fork in the road keep right along the country road. Continue to follow this road which climbs and passes by a solar farm on your right and shortly after starts to run next to the busier A31. At a T Junction turn left and then almost immediately right to join a pavement next to a wider road beside residential properties. Ignore footpaths off to the left and continue to follow the road straight on to arrive at a crossroads by the Cricketers public house.

If you wish to visit New Alresford you can turn left here

At the crossroads continue straight on into another residential street.

After approximately 200 metres where the road turns right continue straight on along a narrower lane. This lane eventually passes between some old watercress beds and then over a ford (there is a footbridge).

The St Swithun's Way then crosses a road to immediately join a footpath which climbs uphill through woodland.

After a short distance and gentle climb the path emerges from the woods near a roundabout on the A31.

Cross the road, with care, to join another country lane opposite heading towards Ovington.

There now follows a long period of road walking. Care should be taken along the parts of the walk as the road is in woodland and can be dark making it difficult for some drivers to see you, especially if they are approaching at speed.

The road enters woodland and winds through the trees. It then drops down and at a bend where the River Itchen comes into view alongside.
At the Bush Inn the road turns sharply left and climbs up into the village of Ovington.
At the next junction the St Swithun's Way turns right to continue along another country lane passing a red telephone box.
Continue to follow this lane, ignoring crossing paths off to the left and right.

After a while the Itchen Way become visible on the right and the St Swithun's Way now merges with this path just before Yaxington Farm.

Approximately 300 metres after passing the farmhouse look out for a stile on the left which now follows a path uphill across a field.
There are views back towards Alresford from here.

The path crosses another stile then turns left along a field edge before turning right to pass through a copse on top of the hill.

After passing through the trees the path joins a wider farm track which heads downhill with large arable fields to the left and a golf course on the right.

The track now climbs and passes by the car park and club house before turning right to head down to the entrance gates of the golf course.

On reaching the road the Way turns left and after a few metres turns right to join a road which passes by the gates to Avington Park on your left.

The road becomes tree lined and crosses the River Itchen before emerging at the unusual church of St John The Baptist in Itchen Abbas.

Immediately after the church the Way turns left to enter a short driveway to houses.

If you wish to visit the Trout Inn you should continue along the road past the church to the junction with the main road. The pub can then be seen opposite to the right.

At the end of the driveway there is a gate to the right which gives access to a narrow enclosed path along the edge of a field.

The path drops down onto another drive where a gate can be seen slightly left which enters a field. Continue straight on along the top right edge of the field with views of the River Itchen below to the left. The field eventually narrows, at the far end there is a gate which gives access to a narrow enclosed path between houses. The path emerges onto a narrow lane and turns left. After 10 metres turns sharp right to climb onto a field edge path. The path enters a large field and turns left where it continues straight on through further fields before passing in front of some pretty cottages at Martyr Worthy.

The Way then passes the Church of St Swithun then through a gate to join another narrow path which emerges into a field. The route turns left and heads downhill towards a hedgerow. At the hedgerow the path turns right along a wide path at first but then along a narrower and sometimes overgrown path to emerge on a road by a house.

Cross directly over the road and over a stile to enter a field. Just before a gate cross over an unusual log stile on the right. Continue along a field edge path keeping a fence to your left.

The noise of the M3 motorway can now be heard as you slowly approach this busy road.
At the end of the field the Way turns left to re-join the river and then passes under the motorway.

After the motorway the route continues to run along the edge of a field climbing towards a road with views of Worthy Park House to the right.
The path emerges onto the road and turns left then after 30 metres left again to leave the road and join a footpath across a grassy paddock passing an old farm building and becoming a woodland path.
The path arrives at a gate with a junction of paths and driveways. At this point The Itchen Way turns left leaving the St Swithun's Way which now continues straight on along a sandy path.

The path emerges on the A33 at Kings Worthy, (this should be crossed with great care) to pass through a gate directly opposite to join a gravel driveway. The path then arrives at St Mary's Church in Kings Worthy where it follows a path through the churchyard to the rear of the church.

On leaving the churchyard the route turns right to pass along a wide paved pavement going through a mixture of residential and commercial properties.

At the end of the path the way passes through a gate turning left and then passing under two bridges carrying the A3411.

After the bridges the path turns left and on arriving at the river right to continue along a narrow path along the riverbank.

The St Swithun's Way continues straight on alongside a wetland area with houses on the outskirts of Winchester now becoming visible ahead.
On reaching the houses the way crosses a stream then continues along the same direction of travel, along a wide path, now keeping the stream on the right.

The path ends at a residential road where it turns right crossing the stream again and then left along a residential road, passing by the King Alfred public house.

At a T-Junction by an old stone gatehouse continue straight on along a tarmac path which turns left to cross the stream once again.

The route now enters another residential street and at the first junction turns right.

Near the end of this second road the way enters a car park on the left and turns right to exit the car park by pedestrian traffic lights. After crossing the road the Way turns right.

At the next junction turn left and keep straight on to enter the retail area of Winchester city centre. Here you should turn right and then left to reach the end of the walk at the entrance to Winchester Cathedral.

There are numerous transport links from Winchester with buses including the 64 from Winchester to Alton and Farnham and rail links to London and Southampton.

St Swithun's Way Approximate Distances

From - to	Miles	Km	Cumulative Total Miles	Cumulative Total Km
Day 1 Total Distance			**12.3**	**19.8**
Day 2 total Distance			**12.2**	**19.4**
Cricketers Alresford to Bush Inn Ovington	1.7	2.3	26.2	41.5
Bush Inn Ovington to Church of St John The Baptist Itchen Abbas	2.0	3.3	28.2	44.8
Church of St John The Baptist Itchen Abbas to Church of St Swithun Martyr Worthy	1.2	2.1	29.4	46.9
St Swithun's Church Martyr Worthy to St Marys Church Kings Worthy	1.6	2.6	31.0	49.5
St Mary's Church Kings Worthy to Winchester Cathedral	2.4	3.9	33.4	53.4
Day 3 Total Distance			**8.9**	**14.2**

Bishops Sutton to Winchester Refreshments

Day 3	Day 3
Ship Inn Bishops Sutton Cricketers at Alresford	
	Pubs, Restaurants & Shops at Alresford
Bush Inn at Ovington (just off route) Trout Inn Itchen Abbas (just off route) Choice of pubs shops and restaurants in Winchester	

Points of Interest and History

After passing the Cricketers public House the St Swithun's Way passes by several old watercress beds. Watercress was transported from Alresford to London along the railway line hence the name "Watercress Line"

Alresford is off route but many of the buildings in the town centre are Georgian in origin and this is worth a visit.

The village of Ovington contains several old houses and lies on the edge of the River Itchen. One of the buildings is the Bush Inn which is a 17th Century building alongside the River Itchen at Ovington.

The St Swithun's Way follows the route of the Itchen Way near Ovington. This is a long distance path of approximately 52 Kilometres (31 Miles) following the River Itchen from its source near Hinton Ampner to Southampton Water. The St Swithun's Way follows the Itchen Way until near Kings Worthy outside Winchester.

After Ovington the route passes through Avington Park Golf course and the entrance to Avington Park House at Itchen Abbas. The original house was built in the 16th century. It was updated and extended in the late 17th century and further changes were made in the late 18th century.

During the summer and on some bank holidays the house is open to the public.

At Itchen Abbas the Church of St John the Baptist is passed. Parts of this church date back to the Norman period however the current building was refurbished and rebuilt in 1867.

At Martyr Worthy is the Church of St Swithun. The church was originally built in the 12th century, however, it was rebuilt and refurbished in 1865. The bell tower was constructed in 1871 this contains 3 bells which date back to the 17th century.

The next church passed on the route is St Mary's at Kings Worthy.

This church was probably originally built in the 12th century and extended in the 15th and 16th centuries but little of those churches remain and the current building was rebuilt in 1864.

The city of Winchester is the county town of Hampshire and was once the capital of Saxon England. Previously the city had been a roman town known as Venta Belgarum.

There is much to see including the Cathedral which is the burial place of Jane Austen who died in the city.

The cathedral is one of the largest in Europe with a long nave and is reputed to have the longest overall length of any European gothic cathedral.

The Buttercross in the centre of the town is believed to date back to the 15th century.

The cathedral is the finish point of the St Swithun's Way. It is also the start point of the South Downs Way, a national trail from Winchester to the Sussex coastal town of Eastbourne.

This walk is approximately 160 Km (100 miles) long.

Printed in Great Britain
by Amazon